LAURA LOMAS

Laura is from Derby. Her plays include *The Blue Road* (youth companies at Dundee Rep/Derby Theatre/Royal & Derngate/ Theatre Royal Plymouth, 2017); *Joanne* (Clean Break/Soho Theatre, 2015); *Bird* (Derby Live/Nottingham Playhouse/UK tour, 2014); *Blister* (Paines Plough/RWCMD/Gate Theatre, 2014); *Open Heart Surgery* (Theatre Uncut/Southwark Playhouse/Traverse Theatre/Soho Theatre); *The Island* (Nottingham Playhouse/Det Norske Oslo, 2009) and *Wasteland* (New Perspectives Theatre/Derby Live, 2009).

Radio plays include *Fragments* (Afternoon Drama, BBC Radio 4), *My Boy* (Somethin' Else Productions/BBC Radio 4), which won Best Drama Bronze at the Sony Radio Academy Awards 2013, and *Lucy Island* (BBC Radio 3, The Wire). Screen credits include *Hanna* (Amazon), *Glue* (E4) and *Rough Skin* for *Coming Up* (Channel 4/Touchpaper), which was nominated for Best British Short at the BIFAs and Best UK Short at Raindance Film Festival.

Other Original Plays for Young People to Perform from Nick Hern Books

100 Christopher Heimann, Neil Monaghan, Diene Petterle

BANANA BOYS Evan Placey

BOYS Ella Hickson

BRAINSTORM Ned Glasier, Emily Lim and Company Three

BROKEN BISCUITS Tom Wells

BUNNY Jack Thorne

BURYING YOUR BROTHER IN THE PAVEMENT Jack Thorne

THE CHANGING ROOM Chris Bush

COCKROACH Sam Holcroft

COMMENT IS FREE James Fritz

EIGHT Ella Hickson

THE FALL James Fritz

GIRLS LIKE THAT Evan Placey

HOLLOWAY JONES Evan Placey

MOTH Declan Greene

OVERSPILL Ali Taylor

PRONOUN Evan Placey

REMOTE Stef Smith

SAME Deborah Bruce

THE SMALL HOURS Katherine Soper

START SWIMMING James Fritz

STUFF Tom Wells

THE URBAN GIRL'S GUIDE TO CAMPING AND OTHER PLAYS Fin Kennedy

THE WARDROBE Sam Holcroft

WHEN THEY GO LOW Natalie Mitchell

Platform

Platform is a series of plays for young actors with all or mainly female casts, which put young women and their stories at the heart of the action – commissioned by Tonic Theatre, published and licensed by Nick Hern Books.

BRIGHT. YOUNG. THINGS. Georgia Christou

HEAVY WEATHER Lizzie Nunnery

THE GLOVE THIEF Beth Flintoff

THE LIGHT BURNS BLUE Silva Semerciyan

RED Somalia Seaton

SECOND PERSON NARRATIVE Jemma Kennedy

THIS CHANGES EVERYTHING Joel Horwood

For more information, visit www.tonictheatre-platform.co.uk

Laura Lomas

CHAOS

NICK HERN BOOKS

London

www.nickhernbooks.co.uk

A Nick Hern Book

Chaos first published in Great Britain in 2021 as a paperback original by Nick Hern Books Limited, The Glasshouse, 49a Goldhawk Road, London W12 8QP

Chaos copyright © 2021 Laura Lomas

Laura Lomas has asserted her moral right to be identified as the author of this work

Cover image: © Shutterstock.com/KRIACHKO OLEKSII

Designed and typeset by Nick Hern Books, London
Printed in the UK by Mimeo Ltd, Huntingdon, Cambridgeshire PE29 6XX

A CIP catalogue record for this book is available from the British Library

ISBN 978 1 84842 987 1

For Tom Wells,
with love and thanks

Chaos was commissioned as part of the 2019 National Theatre
Connections Festival and premiered by youth theatres across
the UK, including a performance at the National Theatre in
June 2019.

Each year the National Theatre asks ten writers to create new
plays to be performed by young theatre companies all over the
country. From Scotland to Cornwall and Northern Ireland to
Norfolk, Connections celebrates great new writing for the stage
– and the energy, commitment and talent of young
theatremakers.

www.nationaltheatre.org.uk/connections

Note on the Text

The play was written for a flexible cast size.

All characters are suggestions – names, genders and pronouns can be changed if necessary, and parts distributed to suit the needs of the company.

Where character names are given it is for ease of reading, and to encourage continuity between scenes – the same actor should play the same part. This should be adhered to if possible.

Where characters are numbered they need not be played by the same actor each time.

The scenes should be symphonic, acting like a piece of music, that grows and evolves over the course of the play.

Companies are encouraged to find the connections. It's nice if stories emerge, it's okay if they don't. Not everything needs to make sense.

Objects can vary – different-sized balls, flowers different colours, etc.

Punctuation is used to indicate rhythm and emphasis. Where there is a notable lack of commas, for example, then it might indicate the speed and urgency with which the line should be delivered.

On pages 65–69, the differences in font size and format is used to indicate speed and emphasis. Companies should feel free to interpret this in any way that feels appropriate to their production, bearing in mind that this section should embody a sense of chaos.

Stage directions can be spoken.

/ marks a point of interruption.

[ ] is to give clarity of intention but where words should not be spoken.

Maybe all the cast are on stage throughout.

Maybe there's music.

Maybe there's movement.

Maybe it's chaotic.

Thanks

I would like to thank Ros Terry, Tom Lyons, Jane Fallowfield, Lucy Morrison, Rachel Taylor, Helena Clark, Debbie Hannan, Lisa Spirling, the cast of the National Youth Theatre who workshopped the play, and everyone who makes National Theatre Connections possible. Special thanks to all the young people who performed it. This play was written for you, and belongs to you.

I would also like to thank my friends and teachers from the youth theatres I attended when I was younger – especially Vicky Harrison, Rebecca Kelly, Laura Moore, James Burke, Rachel Beddow and Lauren Calladine, whose support and friendship have meant the world.

L.L.

Lights up.
A boy is bouncing a ball.
He catches it.
Looks at it.
Lights out.

        Lights up.
        A girl is stood with a bunch of flowers.
        She looks at them.
        Lights out.

Lights up.
A butterfly. With a broken wing.
It flickers on the ground. Electric.
Lights out.

PART ONE

Train

–   So it's Saturday and I'm stood on this train
platform and it's busy, everyone is like packed,
like jammed in, you know an it's early, like twenty
to nine or something, and I'm on my way to work.
The air feels still, almost wet somehow and I
wouldn't normally even be on this platform, cus
normally, my mum, she gives me a lift but since,
she and my dad, since they like...
split, I've been getting the train when I stay at my
dad's and so I'm standing there on this platform,
and I can feel all these bodies...

All these bodies, and it's like they're too close,
somehow, too much, cus I can feel them, it's like
we're one organism, one thing, moving, breathing,
we're that tight and I look to my left, and out the
corner of my eye, I can see this
boy
my age, maybe, or maybe younger, and he's
bouncing this ball
this small, like tiny ball, he's stood at the back of
the platform, listening to music on his
headphones, not really concentrating, and I look at
the clock and it says 8.42, and I know that the
train is coming, cus although I can't see it, I get
that feeling in my legs like vibrating, and the air is
changing, on the platform, it's sort of sucking us,
and I look to my right and there's this woman next
to me

she's holding these flowers, yellow, and she's
moving, like sort of pushing her way, just a little
bit, and I don't think anything, and this boy at the
back is still bouncing this ball, bouncing and

catching, bouncing and catching, and I look at the
clock and it's 8.43 and the train is coming, cus I
can see the lights now it's sort of pulling, and the
feeling in my legs is now in my stomach and the
platform is getting ready, we're like, getting ready
to like fight cus we're not all getting on, and the
boy bounces this ball, and there's suddenly this
moment, this *feeling* where I know, where I know
exactly what's going to... but it's too late, cus the
ball is already... and the train is already... and I
feel the ball hit me and it's like there's a rip, like a
tear in the universe, cus this isn't, none of this is
supposed to... I look up and see this
butterfly
this tiny
fragile
thing
sort of hovering, suspended somehow for a
moment, and then I feel it... the force, and I'm
falling, sort of
spinning through space and I turn my head and
there's this flash, this sort of snap, of something
yellow
and the train it screeches, sort of staggers, and I
look to my right, and the woman
she's not there
the flowers are...
and the boy is looking at his hands, he's looking at
his empty hands...
and the woman she's just... she's just...

Butterfly

Two people. One is bouncing a ball.

1	So it's this idea about the world, okay?
2	Okay
1	And the world is basically *made from chaos*, okay?
2	Okay
1	And if the world is chaos, then it means there's no order, and if there's no order, then it basically means that *anything is possible*
2	Right
1	And if *anything is possible* then it means that *anything could happen,* and if *anything could happen* then it means that *anything might actually happen*, and if *anything might actually happen* then it means that *something will probably happen.*

Beat.

2	Right
1	At any time
2	Okay (*Beat.*) So...
1	So if a butterfly like... *flaps* its wings, in say... Brazil.
2	Okay
1	Then that could cause a massive tornado, in like... Texas

Beat.

2	I don't understand
1	It's complicated

2	But I don't –
1	It's all about consequence
2	Consequence?
1	The input
2	Okay…
1	and the output
2	I don't
1	You can't always predict it
2	So it's
1	Unpredictable
2	Right
1	A change in the initial condition of the system, that disrupts the order
2	disrupts the order / of…?
1	One thing that changes everything
2	One thing that / …
1	Chaos
	Beat.
2	Chaos?
1	Yeah
	Beat.
2	So what do we do?

Hands

DAN *alone. His hands are both bandaged. He removes the bandages from his hands. His knuckles are bruised, bloodied. It's painful.*

EMILY *enters.* DAN *is shocked, embarrassed.*

EMILY   Sorry...

DAN   ...

EMILY   I didn't know anyone was in here, I'm sorry... I'm...

          A beat. DAN *picks up his bag, his bandages.* EMILY *notices his hands.*

EMILY   Wait

DAN   What?

EMILY   Your hands?

DAN   It's nothing.

EMILY   They're bleeding...

DAN   It's nothing.

          He leaves.

Betrayal

IMOGEN, SAL *and* LAUREN *are applying make-up in a mirror. They drink vodka.* BEE *hangs back.*

IMOGEN   So anyway, I was like OMFG, WTF, are you actually kidding me?

SAL   For reals

IMOGEN   Like to see her there

SAL   I know

IMOGEN   An the way she looked

SAL   Seriously

IMOGEN   Like the way she actually looked at me

LAUREN   I know

IMOGEN   With her face

LAUREN   Honestly

IMOGEN   Just standing there. Looking at me. With her face

SAL   For real

IMOGEN   Pass me the vodka

            SAL *does,* IMOGEN *drinks.*

            I said, if you've got something to say you can say it to my face

LAUREN   Exactly

IMOGEN   I said you see this face
            my face
            if you've got something to say you can say it to this face

SAL   Good for you

IMOGEN   An do you know what she said?

            Beat.

            Nothing

SAL	Exactly
IMOGEN	Absolutely nothing
BEE	Do you think she might have been...
LAUREN	Too scared
SAL	Probably
IMOGEN	Too scared to say something, to my face
LAUREN	Coward
IMOGEN	An did you see what she was wearing?
BEE	I... /
LAUREN	I know
IMOGEN	What she was actually wearing
BEE	I...
IMOGEN	An she had the same shoes on as Charlotte, and so Charlotte said she was going to set them on fire when she got in.
LAUREN	Exactly
IMOGEN	Said she didn't care if her mum gave her them for her birthday, she'd just tell her she lost them. She said it was a matter of loyalty
SAL	That's friendship
LAUREN	Exactly
IMOGEN	An did you see her coat?
SAL	Don't
IMOGEN	I swear, I seen it in a charity shop
SAL	I know, don't
LAUREN	It's gross
SAL	So gross
IMOGEN	I can't believe she would do this to me

SAL	I know
IMOGEN	I keep thinking that it's such a betrayal, cus she knew I liked him
BEE	But do you think...
IMOGEN	She knew
BEE	Do you think...
IMOGEN	She a hundred per cent knew because I told her that I like, liked his jumper when we were doing cross-country
SAL	Judas
IMOGEN	I said that to her
SAL	I know
IMOGEN	No word of a lie I said that to her
SAL	I know
IMOGEN	And now they're going out
BEE	Do you think that they might be...
IMOGEN	What?
BEE	Just friends?
	They might be just friends?
	Beat. A look.
IMOGEN	Anyway, I don't even care about him any more
LAUREN	Good for you!
IMOGEN	I think he's gross. I think she's gross. I think they're both gross
SAL	Good.
IMOGEN	I mean, have you seen the state of his hands? What he's done to them.
SAL	It's disgusting

IMOGEN   I mean, who would do that

SAL   Exactly /

BEE   Apparently his dad was like *witness* to this thing
          that happened and he had this like massive / heart
          attack and so

IMOGEN   I don't wanna hear about it /

BEE   I know, but I'm just saying, like /

IMOGEN   I said I don't care, so I don't care, so if I don't
          care, then I don't care /

BEE   I know but...

IMOGEN   I don't care /

SAL   She said she don't care

IMOGEN   I don't

BEE   I know / but

IMOGEN   I don't care

          Pause.

          I keep thinking about them together...

SAL   Oh, don't

IMOGEN   About them kissing...

LAUREN   It's horrible

IMOGEN   I can't get it out my head. You know she was
          supposed to be my friend

SAL   I know

IMOGEN   My best friend

SAL   I thought I was / your

IMOGEN   One of my best friends...

SAL   Right

          Beat.

IMOGEN   Well I hope they're happy together.

LAUREN   Exactly

IMOGEN   I hope they're really bloody happy together

LAUREN   Yeah

IMOGEN   I hope they're like, totally, ridiculously
completely happy together

LAUREN   Me too!

Beat.

IMOGEN   What?

LAUREN   What?

IMOGEN   What d'you mean?

LAUREN   What?

IMOGEN   You want them to be happy together?

LAUREN   I'm just agreeing with you

IMOGEN   I don't actually want them to be happy together

LAUREN   Oh

IMOGEN   I want them to be miserable, Lauren

LAUREN   Oh

IMOGEN   What's wrong with you?

LAUREN   Nothing...

IMOGEN   Pass me the vodka

She does. IMOGEN *drinks.*

Apology

A boy alone.

Another boy arrives.

ALEPH   Hi...

MICHAEL   Hi.

ALEPH   I wasn't sure if you'd...

MICHAEL   I know

ALEPH   Thought you might've... /

MICHAEL   I didn't

                Pause.

ALEPH   How you been?

MICHAEL   Alright.

ALEPH   Yeah?

MICHAEL   Alright...

ALEPH   Good. That's good.

MICHAEL   Yeah

ALEPH   Really good.

                Beat.

                Haven't seen you...

MICHAEL   No

ALEPH   About, or /

MICHAEL   No

ALEPH   Called you

MICHAEL   I know

ALEPH   Few times

MICHAEL   Yeah

ALEPH   Sent messages / and

MICHAEL   I been busy

ALEPH   Yeah /

MICHAEL   Really busy /

ALEPH   Keeping a low profile is it?

MICHAEL   …

Pause.

ALEPH   I wanted to say /

MICHAEL   You don't need /

ALEPH   What happened… /

MICHAEL   You don't need to /

ALEPH   I'm sorry if I /

MICHAEL   It doesn't matter, it's not a big deal

ALEPH   I know but… with the… flowers and…

MICHAEL   Doesn't matter /

ALEPH   Was weird and

MICHAEL   Was fine

ALEPH   Bit weird

MICHAEL   I didn't mind /

ALEPH   But I'm glad you came because I wanted to say, I wanted to say

MICHAEL   I have to go /

ALEPH   But

MICHAEL   I'm sorry

ALEPH   I know but /

MICHAEL   I'm sorry, I have to go, I have to go

Parents

Two girls.

JANE *is bouncing a ball.* SOMALIA *watches her.*

SOMALIA   Are you okay…

JANE *bounces the ball.*

Can you hear me…?

JANE *ignores her, continues bouncing the ball.*

Can you…

JANE   I'm okay

SOMALIA   You're not.

JANE   I am. I'm fine.

SOMALIA   Talk to me

JANE   I don't need to, I'm fine

SOMALIA   Please /

JANE   I'm a bit busy right now, actually, so /

SOMALIA   You're bouncing a ball

JANE   It takes a lot of concentration

SOMALIA   Look at me

JANE *bounces a ball.*

What did she say?

JANE   Nothing

SOMALIA   She must've said something

JANE   She didn't

SOMALIA   So she said nothing. Nothing at all?

JANE   She said that something happened on the train this
               morning and it made her think about things

JANE *bounces the ball*.

SOMALIA   So you just got home from school and he was there?

JANE   Yeah

SOMALIA   Just moved back in?

JANE   Yeah

SOMALIA   Just bags unpacked, just there?

JANE   I said yeah

SOMALIA   An she didn't explain

JANE   No

SOMALIA   She didn't even try to...

JANE   She said she loved him

SOMALIA   But she didn't /

JANE   She said she loved him, it's complicated, she said it's messy, she said it's not straightforward, she said the world doesn't... she said when you're older the world doesn't always make... She said she was doing what felt right... She said to trust her. She said people make mistakes. She said the world is not straight lines. She said it's rough edges. She said it's chaos but we do the best with it. She said she had a feeling in her stomach and it felt like the right one. She said she was doing her best.

SOMALIA   So...

JANE   So.

SOMALIA   That's...

JANE   That's

SOMALIA   Everything?

JANE   Yeah.

Dance 1

A dance routine. It's really boring.

Someone makes a mistake.

Everyone stops. Looks at them.

Protest

CHIARRA *has covered herself in flowers and tied herself to a railing.* MO *talks to her.*

MO	How long will you be there?
CHIARRA	As long as it takes
MO	But it could be forever
CHIARRA	Then I'll stay forever
MO	But really… it could be, forever
CHIARRA	Then I'll stay forever
MO	I'm being serious
CHIARRA	So am I
MO	I'm being properly serious
CHIARRA	Me too
MO	But what are you protesting?
CHIARRA	Everything
MO	But that's too much
CHIARRA	I know
MO	Because it won't change
CHIARRA	It has to
MO	But what if it doesn't
CHIARRA	We have to try
MO	But what do you think will…
CHIARRA	Violence on our streets
MO	I know but
CHIARRA	Rise in sea levels
MO	I know but…

CHIARRA   Nations divided and /

MO   Listen

CHIARRA   Wars and wars and wars and

MO   Yeah, but /

CHIARRA   Government corruption, corporate greed

MO   / Listen

CHIARRA   Police brutality, toxic masculinity, racism!
          Sexism!

MO   Yeah, I know but

CHIARRA   Families torn apart, and /

MO   / Yeah but...

CHIARRA   Ice caps melting, polar bears dying, *people* dying

MO   Yeah, I know but...

CHIARRA   Nuclear weapons

MO   It's not helpful to...

CHIARRA   Fear of women, fear of men

MO   I know, but I don't see /

CHIARRA   Apartheid, genocide, temperatures rising, people
          migrating, the earth revolting, flowers dying, *fish*
          dying, wars breaking out, the planet pulled apart,
          and our hearts breaking / into pieces and

MO   / I know but...

CHIARRA   I saw this thing on a bus, this thing and it changed
          me. It changed me.

          Beat.

          We have to try, don't we, we have to try, we have
          to try

Hope

A BOY *and* GIRL *in a field.*

The GIRL *has a butterfly in her hands.*

BOY   What is it?

GIRL   A butterfly

BOY   Can I see?

            They look at it.

            Its wing is broken

GIRL   I know

BOY   Will it be okay?

GIRL   I don't know.

            She holds it up. Looks at it.

            Maybe

Kiss

Two people. Any gender.

They kiss.

Late

Two sisters waiting at a bus stop.

1	You think he's still coming?
2	Course
1	He's late
2	His bus is late
1	*He's* late
2	Not that late
1	How long do you think you'll wait here before you leave?
2	What?
1	How long do you think you'll wait here, before you leave?
2	What are you talking about?
1	Like an hour?
2	I don't know
1	Like two?
	Said he'd be here at five, didn't he?
2	So?
1	So aren't you worried?
2	No
1	Cus it's already like half past
2	He'll be here
1	But he's late, he's already, like, pretty fucking late so /
2	Why are you here?
1	What?

2	Why are you still here?
1	Waiting with you
2	Shouldn't you go home?
1	No
2	Won't Mum be worrying where you are?
1	No
2	She will be
1	She won't
2	She will
1	She won't
2	She will
1	She won't cus I told her I was hanging out with you for the evening

Beat.

2	What?
1	She said I could
2	I don't want you to
1	Well I am
2	Well, you're not
1	Well I am
2	Well… you're not,
1	Well I am
2	Well… I'm going to have to kill you then

Beat.

1	Okay
2	Fuck's sake
1	Shouldn't swear

2   Fuck off

       Pause.

1   Why do you care so much?

2   What?

1   Why do you care so much, about seeing him,
       when he's late?

2   I don't

1   Do you think he'll bring you flowers?

2   What?

1   Do you think he'll turn up and bring you flowers?

2   Have you been reading my messages?

       Beat.

The Output

Two people. Bouncing balls.

1	The input equals the output
2	What?
1	The input equals the output, it's easy
2	I don't get it
1	It's like if you bounce a ball here, at like a certain speed, a certain sort of force, you can predict where the ball will go
2	I don't understand
1	Like if I bounce it like this

They bounce it.

It lands like that

2	Okay
1	You try

They bounce the ball.

You see?

2	Sort of
1	Try again

They bounce the ball again.

So the input equals the output. It's easy, you just have to understand it /

2	But...
1	What?
2	What if?
1	What?
2	What about wind?

1	What?
2	Wind
1	What about it?
2	What if there's wind?
1	That's not the / experiment
2	Or rain
1	Rain's not really what we're /
2	Or a puddle
1	What?
2	Like if you just bounce it and you bounce it in a massive puddle
1	I don't really know what /
2	Or a storm
1	A storm?
2	Yeah, say there's a storm /
1	A /
2	A Hurricane
1	What?
2	Massive hurricane, say there's a massive hurricane, comes tearing through the country
1	I don't think you're quite /
2	Or a tornado?
1	What?
2	A tornado, ripping up… / everything in its path
1	That's not the experi–
2	Or a tsunami. Massive. The sea swallows the land /
1	I don't think /

2	Forest fires, earthquakes
1	Look, you're not really...
2	Massive earthquake, split in the earth, the whole world falls apart
1	I don't think that... /
2	What if it doesn't?
1	I'm confused
2	I'm just saying, what if it doesn't?
1	What?
2	The input?
1	I don't understand?
2	What if doesn't, equal
1	What?
2	The output.

Depression

1 *has locked themselves in their room.*

2 *stands outside.*

2	You have to come out
1	No
2	You have to
1	No
2	You have to or I'll get your mum
1	I don't care
2	You will do
1	I won't
2	You will
1	I won't
2	You will…
	Nothing.
	I'll get your dad then
1	I'm not bothered
2	Your dad?
1	I don't care
2	But your dad is like [scary]…
1	He's not. And I don't care.
2	What if I just went to get him…
	Nothing.
	If you come out I'll buy you an ice cream
1	I'm okay
2	If you come out we can go down the field

1   ...

2   If you come out, we can ride on our bikes, and we can sit in the grass and we can look at all the *wild flowers* and we can chat about anything, anything you want, and we can nick beers from my dad's garage, and I won't even blame you, I won't even blame you if he finds out, and we can listen to music, and we can practise dance routines, and I won't even laugh when you get it wrong, and we can look at the sky, and try and catch a butterfly and lie on our jumpers, and make daisy chains, and won't you just come out of your room?

Silence.

It's been ages

1   ...

2   Don't you miss it?

1   What?

2   Living?

1   ...

2   Don't you miss it?

Life?

Dance 2

A dance routine. Someone gets it wrong.

Everyone looks at them.

They don't care. They carry on.

Love

A girl talks to others.

AISHA   He said he can't think about nothing else.

He said they were sat there in this field of wild
flowers and he knew, he just knew

He said when he goes to sleep he like, dreams
about him, and when he wakes up, he's the first
thing in his head

He said when he closes his eyes he sees his face
on the back of his eyelids and when he puts his
hand to his heart it's *his* heart he can feel beating.
He says he feels like it's glowing.

He says he can't sleep no more

He says he doesn't eat

He says when he thinks about him, which is *all
the time* he feels like there's butterflies in his
stomach

He says when he opens his mouth they fly out

He says his heart is stretching

He says his heart is a balloon and it's stretching
and when he breathes in, he thinks it might burst,
he thinks it actually might burst, he thinks it might
explode into a thousand million tiny pieces, or *fall
out his chest*, he says his blood is thicker now, he
says his soul is stretching, he says he didn't know
what it was to be a person, before, he says he
didn't know what it was to belong to the universe,
he says the sky is in his cells, he says he knows
infinity, he says it's chaos in his head, he says it's
like he's *spinning round really fast*, he's says it's
like he's in free fall, whirling but everything
makes sense, he says his skin is raw nerves, he
says there's no edges to his body, he says his eyes

are wide open, he says he's different now, he says
it's better, he says it scares him but it's okay, he
says his eyes are the petals of flowers, and his lips
are the wings of a butterfly,

He says his heart might fall out his chest,

He says it's better now. It's better now

Anxiety

Three people. One of them with a football.

1	He's not coming in
2	Why?
1	He wouldn't say
2	What?
1	I asked him, an he told me, said he didn't want to talk about it, said he was going home, he didn't want to say

Beat.

2	When?
1	On the way here
2	What?
1	He text me, on the way here
3	So he'd left?
1	Yeah
2	He'd got up, left the house,
1	Yeah
2	Left the house, got the train
3	Trains were cancelled, he would've got the bus
2	Okay but he left the house, got the bus, he was coming
1	I don't know, I guess so, he just said /
3	That he'd gone home?

Beat.

1	Yeah.

Beat.

2   You reckon something's happened?

1   I don't know

2   You reckon something's happened, on the bus

1   I don't know

2   You reckon something bad's happened on the bus
       and he's not saying

1   I don't know /

3   We should call him

1   I've tried

3   Call him again

1   No.

2   I'll call him

1   He won't pick up

       Beat.

2   If I count to ten and walk backwards then it will
       be okay

1   What?

2   If I count to ten and walk backwards it'll be okay

1   What are you / …

2   Or if I touch every flower, in the park then it'll be
       okay, so…

1   I don't understand

3   Or if you catch a butterfly, if you could like…
       catch a butterfly then I think it'd be okay

2   Yeah?

3   I think if you could catch a butterfly then it'd be
       okay

1   I don't think that would really / [help]

2	I'm not sure I can
3	What?
2	Catch… a butterfly…
3	Oh
1	I don't think we should worry so / much
2	You reckon we should call him?

Beat.

3	I don't know?
2	You think he's okay?

Shoes

A girl enters, she's not wearing shoes.

–   What happened to your shoes?

CHARLOTTE   I set them on fire.

–   Oh. (*Beat.*) Okay.

Spinning

A single person is spinning in circles.

Another person enters. They watch them. They join in.

Race

CHIARRA *speaks to someone else.*

CHIARRA   So I'm on the bus, and it's hot, trains all been
cancelled, so the bus is kinda full. It's busy, but I got
a seat and I'm sitting there, I'm just sitting there, not
really minding nothing, got my headphones in,
listening to something... I can't remember but the
sun's coming in through the window, an it's like
bright, nice, and the bus is calm, you know, it's got
that feeling like when everyone's like
happy
you know, cus it's summer and the windows are
open and there's a breeze, coming in, coming
through, like cool, and the bus stops and you can
feel it shake, sort of shudder a little, and this white
guy gets on, this guy and you can hear him from
down the stairs, cus his voice is kinda loud, and he
sounds maybe... I don't wanna presume, but he
sounds maybe like he's been... drinking which is
weird, cus it's early
and he comes up the stairs, and his face is like
red
you know and he's got this look on it that's like...
you do not wanna... you do not wanna mess, with
him cus the look on his face, is...
an everyone is silent, cus we know... we can just
feel it, the way the air is
and there's this boy, he's sitting, few seats up, and
he's just sitting there, minding his own, and you
can see this guy, he's like looking for... he's really
looking for a fight and this boy, he's not even
thinking... he's like paying him, no attention, like
listening to music
he's got these flowers, in his hand, these
yellow
flowers
and this guy walks up to him and is like
'move'

Beat.

Just like that. And you can see this boy is like
['what?']... cus he's not, he hasn't been
anticipating, you know he's just sitting there, he's
on his way, meet a friend, maybe a date I don't
know, but whatever it is, this isn't what he'd... he
hasn't got time for this and what I haven't told
you is that this boy is black and I don't know if
that's why this guy is going up to him, cus this
guy, he looks... he sort of looks like the type that
might be... the kind of guy that might and I'm
doing all this maths, in my head... and this guy he
just says it, again to the boy, goes
'Move'
an he looks at him, his face close to his face
and the boy goes
'No'

Just like that. Calm, but firm, and the guy... you
can see his face, contorting, cus he's not the kind
of guy who looks like people really say *that* to
him, that often. And so he says it again

'Move'

But this time he spits it, and he's so close to this
boy's face now, and the bus is like charged, all of
us, holding our breath, and we know that this is on
us, you know, that it's on us, to do something, it's
on us. And there's another boy, a different boy
sitting next to me, and you can feel his whole
body *tighten*, he hasn't seen anything like this, he
didn't know the world could look like this, you
can feel it, you can tell
and the boy with the flowers just looks at the guy,
standing there above him, looks at him, calmly

and he reaches out and touches his face, just
gentle, he touches his face

and the guy, the guy he just... he just...

Rage

DAN *walks into a room. He smashes it up.*

He punches the wall.

He hurts his hands.

Rules

1 *explains to a group.*

1   So I was like 'No', but she was like
'Yeah'
So I was like 'You can't'
An she was like
'Well I am'
And I was like 'You're not allowed' and she was
like
'I don't care'
So I was like 'Well what about the rules'
And she was like 'So what?'
So I was like
'If you do it I'm going to call the police' and she
was like 'I don't even care', so I was like...
getting my phone out and she was like
'Are you fucking serious?'
and I was like 'Yeah, cus it's *illegal*,' and she was
like 'What the fuck is wrong with you' and I was
like 'Nothing' and she was like 'Well yeah there
is' and I was like 'Well no there isn't' and she was
like 'Well yeah there is or you wouldn't be being
like this, you know' and I was like 'It's just the
rules, it's just order, it's just the way things
need... it's just the way things are supposed to be,
and maybe you don't think so, but you don't get to
choose so... you know, cus you're not like *God* or
whatever, you just have to accept...' but then she
cut across me and she was like... '*Have you seen
my life, do you even know my life, do you know
anything about my life, does my life look like
order to you, does my life look like rules, does my
life look anything like fucking order to you, do you
know my life, do you know anything about my life*'

An I was like... nothing. I just said nothing

She had scratches on her legs

She looked like she was going to...

I just said... nothing.

I just said...

Scream

Someone screams.

Violence

1   He said since it happened it's changed him, he
said it's different. He said before he used to think
things were possible, he said he used to have
hope.
He said he'd see a butterfly with a broken wing,
and he'd think it'd be... you know... he'd think it
would be okay...
he said he knew things weren't perfect
he knew the input didn't always equal the output
but he thought
he like... felt that people were, fundamentally in
their *hearts* he thought people were *good*... the
world was *good*, that the universe was... even
though it was messy, he said he knew that, but he
didn't think... he said he never felt, before that
people could be so...
he said it's changed him
he said his body is tighter now
and someone brought him flowers but he
couldn't... he said he couldn't even...
he said everything feels like it's hard, and rough
edges
He said his heart is broken
he said it's blasted to pieces
he said he looks at the sky against the trees and
nothing seems right
he said it's different
he said he's changed
he said it's changed him, it's changed him

Universe

1   Well we are essentially the same as stars

2   What?

1   Yeah, I know, it's kind of complicated but it's
           actually true, the inside of our bodies is
           essentially /

2   Stars?

1   Exactly

2   But I don't /

1   Cus when the Big Bang happened it was basically
           this explosion, and everything that had been like
           circling around space for like *billions* of years or
           whatever sort of kind of *clumped together* in this
           explosion of like *heat and light* and you know
           matter, and all that and then the planet was made
           and you know stars, the universe, the *sun*, *et
           cetera*...

2   Et cetera...?

1   Yeah and like, the carbon from that is like in our
           bones you know?

2   What?

1   Yeah, it's fucked up

2   From the Big Bang?

1   Exactly

2   Well...

           Guess that explains a lot

Phone

A girl on the phone. She bounces a ball.

JANE   So I was like 'Babe, you have got to chill out, he
        is not worth it'

        I know

        uh-huh

        I know

        Insane

        I know

        Another phone rings.

        Hang on.

        She answers the other phone.

        Hi…

        Yeah okay

        Yeah okay

        Yeah we had this conversation

        Yeah okay

        Yeah so I know

        Yeah so I don't care

        Because I'm an autonomous, sentient being with
        my own agency

        No I'm not being facetious

        Yeah because I already told you

        Yeah because you know I did

        Yeah when you called me like five minutes ago

        Well, I think you're a dick

        Yeah, well, I think *you're* a dick

Yeah well I think you're a dick too

Yeah well I don't care if you're my mother

Family is a social construct

No, I'm not coming downstairs

Yeah, because you know why

Yeah because you do

Because you do

Because you do

You do

Because I'm not coming downstairs till he is gone

Beat.

Because we spoke about this

Because I don't wanna speak about it again

Because you know what he said to me

Because it's not okay

Because it's not

No I won't open the door

No, I don't want to upset you

No, because you know that

Because you know that

Because you know I love you, it's not about that

Because I can't deal with this no more

Because it hurts me too

Because I'm sorry

Because I'm sorry

Because I'll talk to you later

Because I have to go

Because I have to

Because

Because

Because I'm sorry, because I have to

Because

She puts the phone down.

She picks the other one up, holds it in her hand.

A butterfly flies across the space. She watches it.

PART TWO

Perhaps the pace picks up.

Platform

1   So I'm on this train platform and it's busy,
everyone is like packed... like jammed in... An
it's early,

Eight, maybe eight or nine or something, I can't
remember and I wouldn't normally even be on
this... but it doesn't matter... that's another
story... and I'm standing on this platform, and I
can feel these bodies, moving and I look at the
clock and I know the train is coming, cus although
I can't see it, I can feel it and the air is changing,
it's sort of sucking... and there's this boy at the
back with a ball, a tiny... no wait, a football and
he's bouncing, or is he kicking...? and I look to
my left and there's this woman... She's holding
flowers
these
blue
flowers
and she's pushing, like sort of pushing her way,
just a little bit. And I look at the clock, and the
train is coming and the air is changing, it's sort of
pulling, and the feeling in my legs is now in my
stomach, and the platform is getting ready, it's
getting ready to... [fight], you know cus we're not
all getting on, and I look down and there's this
butterfly, just lying on the ground, its wing looks
like it's broken, and I turn my head and the ball it
goes flying, like spinning, through the air and
there's this flash, like just a snap, the smallest
like... lick of something
Blue

and I see this woman, stumbling and so I
grab her
Just sort of
take her
and I pull her to me
and the train it like screams... it's like so fast it
sort of... screeches and I look at the woman
and my heart is...
and I look at this woman
and the flowers are...
and I hold her
I hold her, the woman, I hold her, I just hold her

Safety

Two girls, outside a house.

JANE   I'm sorry.

SOMALIA   It's okay

JANE   It's late

SOMALIA   It's okay

JANE   I tried to call

SOMALIA   Don't worry

JANE   I didn't know what to do

SOMALIA   You're cold

JANE   He wouldn't stop shouting

SOMALIA   You're freezing

JANE   I could hear him from upstairs

SOMALIA   Your clothes are wet, it's raining

JANE   She was crying, my mum, I could hear her crying

SOMALIA   You're shaking, look at you, you're shaking

JANE   I climbed out the window. I crawled down the garage, I banged my knee on the drop. I landed in the flowers, I scratched my legs on the thorns, I could hear the TV inside the house. He wouldn't stop shouting

SOMALIA   You're okay.

JANE   I didn't know what to do

SOMALIA   You're okay, you're here now. You're okay.

Flowers

Two boys. The school corridor. One is carrying flowers.

ALEPH   I brought you these

MICHAEL   …

ALEPH   To make sure you were okay…

MICHAEL   …

ALEPH   I thought you might like…

MICHAEL   …

ALEPH   Because…

MICHAEL   I can't

ALEPH   But I thought

MICHAEL   I can't

ALEPH   I thought…

MICHAEL   Everything's changed, everything's different

ALEPH   But…

MICHAEL   I'm sorry

ALEPH   Wait..

MICHAEL   I can't

          MICHAEL *leaves*.

Operation

DAN *in a hospital waiting room.*

EMILY *is with him.*

DAN	You don't have to be here
EMILY	I know
DAN	I'm okay on my own
EMILY	I know
DAN	I don't need anyone to... I don't need anyone to like be here, or look after me... or...
EMILY	I know.

Silence.

How long has he been...?

DAN	A while
EMILY	How long?
DAN	A few hours
EMILY	How many
DAN	Six

Short pause.

His heart, they have to take it out. They have to like... open up his chest and take out his heart and reroute his blood, so that they can fix...

EMILY	Are you okay?
DAN	Yeah

It just feels...

EMILY	I'll stay
DAN	You don't have to /
EMILY	I can stay

Short pause.

How is your hand?

DAN   Okay

EMILY   Can I hold it?

DAN   …

EMILY   Can I hold it?

Beat.

DAN   Okay

Platform

Any number of actors.

– So I'm on this train platform and it's busy, everyone is like

– packed

– like

– jammed

– an it's early, eight, maybe

– nine, ten or

– and I wouldn't normally even be on this platform, but

– I'm

– here

– I'm standing

– here

– on this platform, and

– I can feel these bodies,

– moving

– here

– and I look at the clock and I know the train is coming, cus although I can't see it, I can

– feel it

– this butterfly

– and the air is

– changing,

– sort of sucking… and

– there's a boy bouncing

– kicking

–   this ball and

–   I look to my right

–   left

–   and there's this woman… She's holding

–   flowers

–   yellow

–   blue

–   flowers

–   and she's pushing, like sort of

–   shoving

–   her way, and I look at the clock, and the train is
         coming and the air is changing, and the feeling in
         my legs is now in my stomach, and the platform is
         getting ready, it's getting ready and I turn my
         head, I turn my head, I turn my head, / and…

The scenes start to overlap.

Structures

ZARA   Because your structures are not my structures,
         because your body is not the same as my body,
         because my feelings are not the same as your
         feelings, because the things I feel, the things I
         think, the things I want the things I need… Because
         it doesn't fit me. Because it's too small. Because I
         can't grow and I can't be and I can't breathe inside
         your structures, because they're not my structures.
         Because your language doesn't fit in my mouth,
         because your words can't define me, because my
         body is not your body, and my body is my body.
         Because the way I feel is the way *I* feel, because it's
         not straight lines and hard edges. Because there are
         no corners. Because it's curves, and coils and heat
         and colour, because there are things I can't name,

because your language doesn't give me words,
because my feelings are my feelings and my body
is my body and my heart is *so full* it's breaking out,
out of my chest, it's spilling over, because your
language can't define me. And your structures they
don't... they just don't...

Input and the Output

–   The input equals the output

–   So?

–   The input equals the output

–   I don't care /

–   The input equals the output, if I throw this ball
        with a certain speed and a certain force, then it
        lands /

        The ball is taken and thrown away.

Flowers

ALEPH *and* AISHA.

ALEPH   I thought he'd like them

AISHA   I know

ALEPH   I thought he would...

AISHA   I know

ALEPH   I thought it'd make him *feel* the way I feel, the
            way I want him to feel, and we were sitting in this
            field of wild flowers that day and I realised that
            when I'm around him it's like the sky is so much
            bigger, and the world is turning so much faster,
            but now he says that something has changed him,
            it's different, he saw something on the bus and it's
            changed him, his body is tighter, he's different and
            I can't make him feel the way I feel if he doesn't
            feel that way / and so

Anxiety 2

Three people.

1	So what she said was that we're all gonna die
2	True
1	Which she knew, she like… already knew
2	Okay
1	But the thing is, she said she can't stop thinking about it
2	Oh
1	An like, since she's been thinking about it, it's sort of become like *an obsession* it's sort of become like *all* she thinks about
2	Oh right
1	It's sort of become like… her whole brain
2	Right
3	An she started reading about it
2	Oh
3	Yeah, she like, found all these articles, online or whatever
2	Okay
1	About like the climate, and like *drought* and how people are dying cus they haven't got enough water, and like overpopulation and the war in Syria, or the bombs on Palestine, or the violence in the Congo, and the refugees, / like all the millions of refugees, and the waters rising and the forests dying, and the hurricanes, or the earthquakes, and she can't stop thinking about it, she just said she can't stop thinking about it, she said she just can't stop.

Someone spins across the space.

Chaos

The structure falls away. The piece should be as messy and physical and chaotic as it can be.

SO I'm on the bus and it's hot,
the sun's coming in through the
And it's nice, like, summer,
the air is like...   WINDOWS!

– The output

– What?

– It equals?

– What

– The input

WIND

And I feel like my
heart might fall out, I
feel like my heart,
might just fall out my
chest or...

A girl spins through the space.

*Because I can't stop thinking
about it*

And don't you miss it?
Don't you miss it?

You have to come out

NO!

These [flowers] are for you

– What is it?

– A butterfly   Do you think it will be
okay?

– Its wing is broken   <u>AN EARTHQUAKE</u>

– Will it be okay?

> *A boy walks into a room, he smashes*
> *it up*
> *he hurts his hands*
> *His heart falls out his chest*

Because I feel like it's glowing

My heart!

Many balls bouncing.

I feel like it's glowing

Because the universe, is chaos, and

It rains.

The ruling principle is...

SOMEONE SCREAMS!   A Tornado

The carbon from the Big Bang is in our bones! Did you know that? We're made of stars

> She said she loved him, it's complicated, she said
> it's messy, she said it's not straightforward, she
> said the world doesn't... when you're older the
> world doesn't. She said she was doing what felt
> right... She said to trust her. She said people make
> mistakes. She said the world is not straight lines.
> She said it's rough edges. She said it's chaos but
> we do the best with it. She said she had a feeling
> in her stomach and it felt like the right one. She
> said she was doing her best.

Someone opens their mouth –
butterflies fly out.

– Because we have to try

– I know but /

Someone bounces a
ball.

– We have to try

The ice caps will melt,
the polar bears will die

The rivers will dry up

Two people kiss

A field of wild flowers.

The land will crack   The fish will die

The waters will rise

A dance routine. Everyone gets it
wrong. No one cares

Someone cries

The crops will die, and the temperature will rise,
and the people will migrate, and the fuel will run
out, and the earth will revolt, and the fish will die,
and the flowers will dry out, and the wars will
break out, and the planet will be pulled apart, and
our hearts will break into pieces /

*And do you know my life, do you even know my life, do you know
anything about my life, does my life look like order to you, does
my life look like rules, does my life look anything like order to you,
do you know my life, do you know anything about my life /*

Someone is sick

You have to come
out

No

You have to

No

I'll call your mum

No

I'll call your dad

I don't care

EARTHQUAKES
IN CHINA

**My soul is
stretching**

A BOY BOUNCES
A BALL

And will you hold
my hand?

Because I worry
about the ozone
layer

And I worry about
the Sea

And I worry about
the fish

And I worry about
the wars wars wars

And I worry about
the people, all the
people people

*Will you hold
my hand?*

*Will you hold my
hand?*

*Will you hold my
hand?*

*And it feels like it's
just everything
everything
everything
everything
everything
everything
everything
everything
everything
everything
everything
everything*

everything
everything
everything
everything

PART THREE

The space should suddenly feel very calm, still even.

The speaker should be the same as in the very first monologue.

Over the next the space gets slowly lighter.

–   So it's Saturday.

Summer.

I'm in the car with my mum, cus... I stayed at hers last night

And we're driving.

She's giving me a lift to work.

It's early, but... not too early. The sun is up.

The traffic is moving, slowly, calmly

And everything is easy

It feels kind of peaceful

And I look out the window and... I start to notice the world

a boy with a ball

a woman with some flowers

a little girl spinning in circles, just on her own

and I know it sounds weird but as we're driving I start to imagine all the possibilities, you know? All the different things that can happen, in a day, or a moment, or a life, or a world. And I know this will sound strange, but it's like I start to see it, it's like I start to see this map of everything, everything that we're made of and how everything is connected and what it means and how it fits or

doesn't fit, and how this map is chaos, like in my
head this map is just total, complete... you know?
but it's beautiful

and I have this thought that maybe it's us, like the
inside... somehow, that maybe it's us

and I know it doesn't make sense, but I know that
it's...

right

somehow. It's right.

And we drive past the train station, and I look out
the window.

Me and my mum

We drive. We just keep driving.

The stage should now be very bright.

In the light we can see everyone. The whole cast.

A field of wild flowers.

Everyone holding bouncing balls.

A butterfly flies past.

The End.

www.nickhernbooks.co.uk

facebook.com/nickhernbooks

twitter.com/nickhernbooks